VICTORY
over
SATANIC DREAMS

 Dr. D.K. Olukoya

© 1996 - Dr. D. K. Olukoya - Victory Over Satanic Dreams

A *publication of:*
Mountain of Fire and Miracles Ministries

Lagos, Nigeria Address
13, Olasimbo Street. off Olumo Road,
(By UNILAG Second Gate)
Onike, Iwaya
P. O. Box 2990, Sabo, Yaba, Lagos.

London Address
Battersea Chapel,
WYE Street,
Battersea,
London SWII 2SR
☎ 0171-2286407

All rights reserved No part of this publication may be reproduced, stored in a retrieval system, or be transmitted, in any form, or by any means, mechanical, electronic, photocopying or otherwise without the prior written consent of the publisher.

It is protected under the copyright laws.

ISBN 978-0692340035

Typesetting, Designing and Printing at
MFMPRESS
13, Olasimbo Street, off Olumo Road,
by Unilag 2nd Gate, Onike, Yaba, Lagos, Nigeria.

All Scriptures are quoted from the King James Version of the Bible.

Second Edition May 1996

Cover Designed by: Sister F. Olukoya

Other Books by Dr. D. K. Olukoya
* Students In The School Of Fear .
* The Vagabond Spirit
* How To Obtain Personal Deliverance
* Power Must Change Hands
* Breakthrough Prayers For Business Professionals
* Pray Your Way To Breakthroughs (Third Edition)
* Spiritual Warfare And The Home
* Victory Over Satanic Dreams (Second 'Edition)

This and other books by Dr. D. K. Olukoya can be obtained from:
MFM BOOK SHOP
13, Olasimbo Street, off Olumo Road, by Unilag 2nd Gate,
Onike, Yaba, Lagos, Nigeria.
Or any other leading Christian Book Stores.

DEDICATION

This Book is dedicated to all Members of the Council of The Mountain of Fire and Miracles Ministries. God will remember them for good.

PREFACE

Victory Over Satanic Dreams is like a Watchman cry. Many experiences that have put people in life-time problems could have been avoided if they had understood some signals. No wonder the Prophet Hosea exclaimed: "My People are destroyed for lack of knowledge (Hosea 4:6). Everybody dreams at one time or the other, but many are not knowledgeable enough to understand that the things seen in the physical had existed first in the spiritual realm.

The HolySpirit through this Book will open your eyes unto the actual root of bondage which you think came suddenly. Dreams may be more important than you think.

All the examples contained in this Book are practical experiences of particular individuals. That prevention is better than cure is still a wise saying that needs to be adhered to.

I welcome you to a new mountain top life of Victory Over Satanic Dreams.

Pastor Ayo OIuwatosin
Co-ordinator Tracts and Publications Department
Mountain Of Fire And Miracles Ministries
Lagos:

v

VICTORY OVER

SATANIC DREAMS

INTRODUCTION

Dreaming is a natural way in which the spirit world breaks out into our lives.

Dreams can be described as the dark speech of the spirit. Dreams are a means of revelation. Unfortunately, modern men and women have chosen to either ignore dreams altogether or to fear that an interest in them is lack of civilization. The fact is that if we would listen, dreams can help us find increased spiritual victory and help.

Once we have the revelation that dreams can be a key to unlocking the door to the spirit world, we can take some vital steps. First, we can specifically pray inviting God to inform us through our dreams. Secondly, we should declare war when dreams are used against us. Third, we should learn how to interprete dreams. The best way to discover the meaning of dreams is to ask the Holy Spirit.

It is worthy of note that God promised that He would speak to His people by dreams in the last days. Acts 2: 17: *"And it shall come to pass in the last days, saith God, I will pour out of my Spirit upon all flesh: and your sons and your daughters shall prophesy, and your young men shall see visions and your old men shall dream dreams"*. Therefore, our dreams need to be studied and analysed with a view to decoding their messages.

I want you to speak to the Lord now. Ask the Lord to make this day a special moment in your life. Tell Him to make this day a day you will never forget.

Let us pray.

"Our Father and our God, we thank You for the demonstration of Your power. We thank You for the

2

wonders You have done in the past. We thank You for what You are doing right now. Thank You for what you will continue to do. Thank You because You have determined to bless us. We are not candidates for destruction. We are candidates for blessing. We thank You because whatever good things we have not experienced before this time will be manifested now. We know that You are working out our miracles by Your power and Your grace. O Lord, accept our thanks in Jesus' name. Right now, Holy Father, I commit this hour into Your hands. I pray that as many as are reaching out to You by faith now will not go empty handed, in the name of Jesus. Show forth Your glory. Let heaven come into our souls and hearts so that we will not remain the same after this encounter with You. Wonderful God, I pray that You open our spiritual ears today. Teach us from Thy throne in Jesus' name. O Lord, any problem that has followed anybody up till this point, we command the problems to be buried in the name of Jesus. We thank You because you have answered. In Jesus' name we pray. (Amen)

I have a somewhat difficult task at hand. But I know that the Lord will help me. I want you to be very attentive. I am sharing a life-changing truth with you today.

The message contained in this booklet is similar to a booklet I titled: Breaking Witchcraft Curses.

By the grace of God, we are looking at an important topic which, I believe, will lead to your total deliverance. The problems of most people can be traced to our subject of consideration. I am, therefore, speaking to you on: "Victory Over Satanic Dreams".

You have to read carefully and pay attention to the entire content of this booklet. Do not allow sleep or any distractions to rob you of the blessings of this booklet. The

3

enemy of your soul will try and prevent you from reading this book with full concentration. I know that the devil does not want you to experience victory over satanic dreams. But do not worry: the devil has been defeated for you.

SATANIC STRATEGY

There is no other passage to turn to for a proper understanding of victory over satanic dreams than Matthew 13:25: *"But while men slept, his enemy came and sowed ..."*.

A dream is a natural way in which the spiritual world breaks into our lives. Dreams can be a key to unlocking the door to the inner world. Dreams have been referred to as the speech of the spirit. Unfortunately modern Christians have tended to either ignore dreams altogether or take them as playthings.

Every normal person is supposed to sleep. God in His own Wisdom has designed this for man. Everything which God has designed for man is for a good purpose. But the problem is that the enemy goes into every good thing and corrupts it. The devil turns anything that should be a friend of man into an enemy. Dreams play an active role in the lives of men and women. Unfortunately, the problems in the lives of most people start with instances of satanic dreams.

People face two types of danger. One, a lot of people are so deep in spiritual sleep that they never remember what they dreamt about when they wake up. This is the twin danger; when somebody dreams and forgets everything, he stands the danger of missing an important message or ministration from God if He was the One speaking through the dream.

4

Two, if the enemy is carrying out an evil activity and you forget the dream, you also face the danger of remaining under bondage. If you are fond of forgetting dreams on a regular basis, you have a very serious problem.

I remember the case of a sister who came to the church during the time we were having a seventy-day fasting and prayer session. We had a session tagged: "Know The Secrets". She went to the Lord and requested to know certain secrets. As she was praying, God opened her eyes and she found herself before a great king who told her: "Be careful about that church you are attending; I have only allowed you to go there because I know that you will never become a genuine member of the church". Then she woke up. She came to me for counselling and told me about the dream. I told her: "You have a strange king ruling over your life. Jesus is the only true King. You have a demonic king to dethrone in your life. You must dethrone that king and lift Jesus up". She started praying, saying; "You strange king, be dethroned in the mighty name of the Lord Jesus Christ " She was not fully aware of the problem she was bringing upon herself. The same night she prayed, she found herself before the throne of that same king. The king was angry. He confronted her and said: "What kind of nonsense is this? I know how to deal with you. I will remove your spiritual memory so that whatever you see or hear in a dream will never be remembered". Since that day, the sister just sleeps and wakes without remembering any dream she had. As a result of her spiritual level, the devil kept on doing great havoc against her life without her knowledge. This sister eventually declared war against her oppressors and dethroned the foreign king. There is a double danger here. You need to pray against this type of problem.

5

DEMONIC ATTACKS

Sometimes, people experience the manifestation of what evil powers have done in the dream.

Most of the time, what happens in the realm of the dream happens in the physical realm. Another sister dreamt about somebody who was defecating on her head. She was worried. Unfortunately, she belonged to a fellowship where spiritual warfare is not taught. Since that day, her husband began to hate her. That marked the beginning of the ruin of her marriage.

Occasionally, satanic agents force people to eat in the dream. Problems often start with such strange dreams. The Bible says: *"My people are destroyed for lack of knowledge"* (Hosea 4:6).

Many people have suffered terribly as a result of ignorance of what the devil does in dreams. Many people have fallen prey to the enemies through dreams. Many have been made to believe lies and errors through satanic dreams. The enemy has used dreams to confuse a lot of people in their marital, business, financial and spiritual matters.

TYPES OF DREAMS

A dream may come in form of an activity which the dreamer is involved in. Apart from being an activity, a dream may come as an event. For example, the dreamer may find himself sitting down and watching the television. Sometimes a dream could be centered on something which has occurred or something which is about to occur. The dream may also be a message to a particular person. Some people also dream strange dreams inside a dream. Of course, that is strange. Such people need prayer. A dream sometimes comes as an attack on the dreamer. Some forces may start fighting against you in a dream. Whichever is your dream, the spirit world is trying to have an impact on your life.

SOURCES OF DREAMS

Therefore, dreams are generally a film of occurrences in the spiritual realm. Before we dig deep into the revelation concerning dreams, we want to take an incisive look into the sources of dreams. Where does dream comes from?

Dreams may come from God. This is demonstrated in Joseph's life.

"Now Israel loved Joseph more than all his children, because be was the son of his old age: and be made him a coat of many colours. And when his brethren saw that their father loved him more than all his brethren, they hated him, and could not speak peaceably unto him. And Joseph dreamed a dream, and be told it to bis brethren: and they hated him yet the more. And be said unto them, Hear, I pray you, this dream which I have dreamed: For, behold, we were binding sheaves in the field, and, lo, my sheaf arose, and also stood upright; and, behold, your sheaves stood round about, and made obeisance to my sheaf" (Genesis 37:3-7).

This account reveals that God revealed Joseph's life story to him in a dream.

The fact that God speaks to people through dreams is clearly enunciated in Numbers 12:6.

7

"*And He said, Hear now My words: If there be a prophet among you, I the Lord will make Myself known unto him in a vision, and will speak unto him in a DREAM*".

Another popular passage in the Bible further clarifies this point:

"*And it shall come to pass afterwards, that I will pour out My Spirit upon all flesh, and your sons and your daughters shall prophesy, your old men shall DREAM DREAMS, your young men shall see visions*" (Joel 2:28).

This same verse was also quoted in Acts 2:17.

The Bible says:

"*The prophet that hath a dream, let him tell a dream; and he that hath My word, let him speak My word faithfully. What is the chaff to the wheat? saith the LORD?*" (Jeremiah 23:28).

A NEW TESTAMENT DREAM

This passage shows us that a God-appointed prophet could have dreams. You might say that this is an old testament passage. But what will you say when you read a New Testament passage?:

"*And being warned of God in a DREAM that they should not return to Herod, they departed into their own country another way. And when they were departed, behold, the angel of the Lord appeareth to Joseph in a DREAM, saying, 'Arise, and take the young child and his mother, and flee into Egypt, and be thou there until I bring you word: for Herod will seek the young child to destroy him'. When he arose, he took the young child and his mother by night, and departed into Egypt"* (Matthew 2:12-14).

So, how did God speak to Joseph? God spoke to him through a dream. God speaks to people in dreams in order to instruct them concerning what to do. God also speaks to people in dreams in order to warn them. Let us look at Job 33:14-16:

"For God speaketh once, yea twice, yet we perceiveth it not. In a dream, in a vision of the night, when deep sleep falleth upon men, in slumberings upon the bed; then He openeth the ears of men, and sealeth their instruction".

God speaks to people in their dreams. Sometimes, people are too noisy. God, therefore, chooses to speak to them through dreams. Many people have formed the habit of tuning to local and foreign radio stations immediately they wake up in the morning. So when they go to work they also face the "noise" of traffic jam. Immediately they got to their office, they are bombarded with the noise of idle talk. When they close from work and they are on their way home, it is noise again. As soon as they get home, it is the noise of T.V.. So, the only time they experience any form of quietness at all is in the night when they are sleeping. That is the only time God can gain their attention if He wants to speaks to them.

THE PURPOSE

God can warn of an impending danger through a dream like He did to Joseph, the earthly father of Jesus.

He can also show you the blue-print for your life like He did to Joseph. God can also use a dream to rebuke a person. If the person complies with God's word, there will be grace and mercy.

God can also use dreams to reveal the plan of your life to you like He did in the case of Solomon.

"In Gibeon, the Lord appeared to Solomon in a dream by night: and God said, Ask what I shall give thee: And God said unto him, Because thou has asked this thing, and hast not asked for thyself long life; neither hast asked riches for thyself, nor hast asked the life of thine enemies; but has asked for thyself understanding to discern judgement: . . . And if thou wilt walk in My ways, to keep My statutes and My commandments, as thy father David did walk, then I will lengthen thy days. And Solomon awoke: and, behold, it was a dream . . ."(1 Kings 3:5,11-15).

God can use dreams to encourage a person like He used it to encourage, direct, instruct and make covenants with Bible characters. There are many examples in the Bible.

Pharaoh dreamt about impending famine. The wise men who visited and gave gift to Jesus when He was born were also directed through a dream.

Paul had a dream in which he was told: "Come over to Macedonia and help us." Pilate's wife also had a dream which made her to warn her husband to wash his hand. clean from unlawful persecution of Jesus.

All these are practical examples.

Has God given you any dream about your life? Pray until it comes to pass. Remember, God does not give bad dreams to His Children. He only gives good dreams. The Bible says:

"For I know the thoughts that I think toward you, saith the Lord, thoughts of peace, and not of evil, to give you an expected end" (Jeremiah 29:11).

Every God-given dream is for your good. If God has warned you through a dream to take an important or urgent step in your life, you must obey promptly. Please do so. In conclusion, divine dreams can be divided into four kinds (1)dreams of instruction or teaching (2)dreams of the prophetic nature (3)dreams of warning (4)dreams of encouragement.

MENTAL DREAMS

Dreams also come from man. People dream about what they are pre-occupied with in their day-to-day activities:

"For a dream cometh through the multitude of business; and a fool's voice is known by multitude of words" (Ecclesiastes 5:3).

Again the Bible says:

"For in the multitude of dreams and many words there are also divers vanities: but fear thou God" (Ecclesiastes 5:7).

When a dream comes from man, God has nothing to do with it. Neither is the devil behind dreams which emanate from the mind of man. This is made very clear in the Scriptures:

"It shall even be as when an hungry man dreameth, and, behold, he eateth; but he awaketh, and his soul is empty: or as when a thirsty man dreameth, and, behold, he drinketh; but he awaketh, and, behold, he is faint, and his soul hath appetite . . ." (Isaiah 29:8)

You only dream about what occupies your mind throughout the day. When you fill a glass with water, a little tilt will spill some water. If your heart is brimful with a particular thought, such thoughts will be replayed in your dreams. Those who have given themselves to fornication and all forms of immorality, will dream about it. Sad people will always dream about tragedy. If you read a bad book before going to bed, you are likely to see horrible pictures of what you read in your dream. If you read an occultic book, you will dream of weird and occultic things. If you watch a terrible and corrupting television programme, you will see the same things in your dream.

INFLUENCE

If you are a believer who is fond of counting his woes, tragedies and misfortunes, you will do the same in your dreams. If your dreams are completely taken over by worldly things and you are always dreaming of dancing at parties, you need to repent; your dreams are reflections of your state of mind. Fleshly or carnal dreams can be so deceptive, especially when you have not crucified your flesh. To a large extent, if you are filthy, you will have filthy dreams. If you are holy, you will have heavenly and God-honouring dreams. Confused people have confusing and senseless dreams. Demonic people have demonic dreams. Sick people generally dream about sickness. There is a fitting example in the Book of Job:

"Now a thing was secretly brought to me, and mine ear received a little thereof. In thoughts from the visions of the night, when deep sleep falleth on men. Fear came upon me, and trembling, which made all my bones to shake" (Job 4:12-14).

Job dreamt about fear, trembling, and the shaking of his bone when he was sick. Your physical condition goes a long way in influencing your dreams. That is why a banker would dream of counting money.

In the same vein, a post office staff may always dream of letters and stamps. You do not need to bother about these types of dreams. They only reflect your physical or emotional condition.

However, there is a class of dreams which should attract the attention of everyone. This class of dreams has ruined many people's lives. In particular, I am talking about SATANIC DREAMS A dream could come from the devil. Demons have infiltrated into the lives of men and women through dreams. This is the area I really want to explore in this booklet.

THE DEVIL'S MOTIVE

The strategy of the devil is to cause calamity and destruction. His purpose is to inflict sickness on people, terrify men and make evil covenants with innocent souls. His sole aim is to kill and destroy. He also attempts confusing men and makes them to take wrong decisions. The devil is a deceiver. He deceives through dreams. He gives people confusing images in their dreams. He might make a person see a man with white garment in the dream and make him to conclude that God is speaking to him. This reminds me of a brother who was praying and all of a sudden, someone walked up to him and told him to stop praying. He was baffled when the personality added: "That prayer is too much". The Brother paused and wondered why Jesus would ever ask him to stop praying. However, the Brother looked closely and to his surprise, he found dirty spots all over the garment of the strange personality.

His eyes got opened. Then the Brother shouted: "You are an agent of the devil. You are not from God!" The white garment man disappeared. The devil was trying to deceive him. This is how the devil darkens the vision of many prophets. After such a deceptive vision, they generally relapse into strange doctrines. They go about saying: "God told me that I should not eat any food cooked by a woman. God also told me that I should tear up my Bible and eat it." You must be careful when you hear or see such things. The devil is always looking for people to deceive.

DIRECT SATANIC ATTACKS

Besides leading people into error and bondage through dreams, the devil also afflicts people directly. All the dreams about accidents, attacks, carrying loads, closed doors, youth growing old, chains in the neck, closed Bibles are all symbolic. They represent one form of satanic attack or the other. If you also find yourself drinking concoctions or poison in your dreams, you are surely under attack. If you dream of your property being confiscated or if you see a coffin in your dream, the devil is at work. Those who dream of seeing themselves being lost in the forest, those who see black shadows in dreams and those who see people running after them are also experiencing some forms of satanic attack. Again, if you find yourself screaming in your dreams something is surely amiss. Those who are fond of eating assorted foods in the dream are most probably under attack. So are those who see snakes, water, dead relatives, "spirit husbands", "spirit children" and masquerades. These all have connotations in the spirit world. The devil uses them as points of contact.

The list is almost endless. The Bible talks of "Depths of

14

Satan". The devil has many mysterious ways of afflicting people. Sweating profusely in the dream, labouring as in pregnancy, serving food to people you do not know, attending strange meetings in the dreams, being attacked by crocodiles, cats, dogs and lions and other strange occurrences in dreams are all part of Satan's method of enslaving and destroying people.

SPIRITUAL WEAPONS

When unchecked, Satan uses the dream world to his advantage. He has a very subtle trick. What he does is that he allows two or three bad dreams to come to pass; then he proceeds to make people to believe that every bad dream must come to pass.

When such people come to me for counselling and prayer, they often tell me: "Sir, my case is very urgent. Whenever I have a dream, it always come to pass. I am afraid this dream will also come to pass". It is clear that people with this kind of mind-set have been deceived by the devil. You must not allow the devil to deceive you. That is why you should learn how to make use of spiritual weapons. Those who come under our teaching and ministration regularly are always taught the effective use of weapons of spiritual warfare. You need to know how to make use of the weapons which God has given you. But what does the Bible say about these weapons?

"For the weapons of our warfare are not carnal, but mighty through God to the pulling down of strongholds" (2 Corinthians 10:4).

THE NAME OF JESUS

The most powerful weapon which is available for our use against satanic dreams is the name of JESUS. The Bible says·

"The name of the LORD is a strong tower: the righteous runneth into it, and is safe" (Proverbs 18:10).

No matter how terrible you are attacked in your dream, if you can still have the consciousness to call the name of Jesus, no power will be able to overcome you.

You can use the name of Jesus to overcome every satanic warfare in the dream. But if you call the name of Jesus and evil powers refuse to obey, then there is a sin in your life. Something is surely wrong somewhere. There is no other explanation. You cannot blame other person. Sin will render your prayer ineffective. You, therefore, need to know the power in the name of Jesus.

Perhaps, you are wondering: why is it that sometimes when I am dreaming, I do not even remember to call the name of Jesus? It is because the name of the Lord Jesus has not yet entered into your spirit. If you keep on repeating a particular word or phrase for ten hours, you will discover that you might continue repeating the word when you are asleep, because it has entered into your subconscious. If you are always calling the name of Jesus in real life, you will find it easy to call His name in your dreams. In the same way, if you are always making use of bad vocabulary, you will need deliverance. But when your vocabulary is positive and words like: "Jesus, Glory be to God, God is good and the goodness of the Lord" are always on your lips, you will repeat the same words in your dreams.

THE BLOOD OF JESUS

The Blood of Jesus is another weapon you can use against satanic dreams. This is clearly stated in the Bible:

"And they overcome him by the Blood of the Lamb, and by the word of their testimony; and they loved not their lives unto the death" (Revelation 12:11).

The Blood of Jesus is a very powerful weapon. Remember, it is written:

"And the blood shall be to you for a token upon the houses where ye are: and when I see the blood, I will pass over you, and the plague shall not be upon you to destroy you ..." (Exodus 12:13).

THE FIRE OF GOD

The Fire of God is another weapon against demonic dreams. This may sound like a strange weapon, but earnest students of the Bible and matured students in school of spiritual warfare are conversant with this weapon. The Bible declares :

"For behold the LORD will come with fire, and with His chariots like a whirlwind, to render His anger with fury, and His rebuke with flames of fire" (Isaiah 66:15).

The Bible also stated that God is a consuming fire. So it is clear that you can call the fire of God to consume, burn or roast all forms of satanic dreams. The Word of God is filled with wonderful revelations concerning our spiritual weapons. You need to search the Word of God for light and guidance. You also need to memorize scriptures to effectively deal with the enemy each time he comes against your life. There is no short cut to victory.

17

If you fail to learn enough scriptures, you might be confused at the hour of battle. It is never too late. You can start to memorize scriptures today. The average Christian ought to be able to recite at least fifty memory verses. It is rather unfortunate that some people find it difficult to commit Bible verses to memory. Such people are, however, quick to memorize the wordings of worldly music. This is the work of the enemy.

ANGELS OF GOD

Another strange but powerful weapon which God has given every believer are angels. Angels play a prominent role in the battles which the believer faces. The Bible says:

"There shall be no evil befall thee, neither shall any plague come nigh thy dwelling. For He shall give His angels charge over thee, to keep thee in all thy ways" (Psalm 91:10,11).

Again the Bible says:

"Let them be confounded and put to shame that seek after my soul: let them be turned back and brought to confusion that devise my hurt: . . . . Let their way be dark and slippery and let the angel of the LORD persecute them" (Psalm 35:4-6).

Angels are part of our weapon for spiritual warfare. Some believers think that we should never fight against or deal with the enemy. Some people believe that we should just fold our hands since God know how to give us victory. But there is nothing wrong if a Christian prays and commands that certain spirits should be bound. You have the weapons. Why not use it? There is nothing wrong with commanding the thunder and the lightning of God to blast the enemies of your soul. This is a very effective weapon. Also, there is

18

nothing wrong if a believer commands that the whirlwind of God should scatter the enemy's devices against you. There is also nothing wrong if a believer chooses to apply the arrow and the spear of God against dark powers. There is nothing bad, too, if a believer commands the tempest of God to deal with all satanic agents. There is just nothing wrong with a believer who prays like the psalmist, especially after being harassed or attacked in a dream.

COSTLY IGNORANCE

There are weapons every believer who wants to enjoy personal victory must learn to use. This is very important for members of churches where almost nothing is said about spiritual warfare. Either you like it or not, you have to fight battles. If you despise the weapons of your warfare, you are seeking your defeat. You cannot give any excuse for your defeat. The weapons are there in the Bible. If your personal victory is important to you, you will thoroughly search God's word and make use of the weapons fashioned for you by God.

However, you must be ready to forget your traditional church beliefs and embrace the teaching on spiritual warfare. Some believers want to appear more righteous than God. But see what the Bible says:

"My defence is of God . . . and God is angry with the wicked every day. If he turns not, he will whet His sword; He hath bent His bow, and made it ready. He hath also prepared for him the instruments of death; He ordaineth His arrows against the persecutors" (Psalm 7:10-13).

"The heathen are sunk down in the pit that they made: in the net which they hid is their own foot taken. The LORD is

known by the judgement which He executeth: the wicked is snared in the work of his own hands . . ." (Psalm 9:15,16).

"The wicked in his pride doth persecute the poor: let them be taken in the devices that they have imagined" (Psalm 10:2).

"Stir up thyself, and awake to my judgement, even unto my cause, my God and my Lord. Let them be ashamed and brought to confusion together that rejoice at mine hurt: let them be clothed with shame and dishonour that magnify themselves against me" (Psalm 35:23,26).

We must learn to use the various weapons put at our disposal by God. Why? Sources of problems differ. Sources of attack also differ. But praise God! The Lord has given us all the weapons we would ever need for the battle of life.

USE APPROPRIATE WEAPONS

Although God has given us many weapons, certain spirits will respond to a particular weapon while another weapon may not have any effect over them. This reminds me of the story of somebody I prayed for a long time ago. Before I prayed for him, somebody came and issued a command saying: "Fire of God, burn this evil spirit". Another person got there and said: "No that is not the right method". He then prayed: "The blood of Jesus! get into this situation". Then the problem started. The person being prayed for began to speak Latin. Imagine a fourteen year-old boy who has never gone outside the country speaking fluent Latin!

The boy later confessed that the spirit troubling him came from Rome. No wonder, he had killed his father and mother. This is why we must study the different methods of

20

dealing with demonic problems.

Certain stubborn spirits may require a combination of weapons. For examples, if you had a dream in which somebody came to take your property away, you should command that the Holy Spirit should reach out for the robber. You should also command the thief to appear with your property. Then bind the spirit behind the thief. You can also release the thunder, the arrow and the sword of God into the body of the thief. You can ask that the arrow remains there permanently. Then, you should collect your property. Finally, cover your property with the blood of Jesus.

Perhaps, you dreamt of seeing masquerades, you can command the consuming fire of the Almighty God to roast the masquerades. You can also send them to the place of torment. The masquerade is an embodiment of evil spirits in our environment.

It is very easy to know when a dream is from God, or if it is from the devil. If a dream comes from God you will be normal when you wake up, but if it is a satanic dream, mysterious things will begin to happen to you. It will be accompanied by feelings of confusion and emptiness. It will leave you unconscious. However, if you are attacked in a dream, never panic. Do not be afraid. Immediately you are afraid, evil strategies will begin to work against your life.

Perhaps, you may wonder how I have been able to understand certain mysteries of satanic invasions through dreams. But I doubt if you will wonder how a tested war general has mastered warfare. You will surely not wonder how such an army general has succeeded in demonstrating a mastery over the position, the weapons and the strategies of enemy forces. Again, the weapons the army general might use may be strange to you, all the same, he knows that his terminologies are real. His experience, his endowments and his personal experience would have made him a veteran. In the same vein, you should expect a servant of God who has been incubated and trained by God to understand the mysteries and the interpretations of demonic symbols used in dreams. As you go through the list of the following symbols and meanings, you may come across certain revelations which may not be familiar to you.

What you are about to discover will make you to be more conscious of the fact that the devil is a blood-thirsty warrior who also carries his battle to the realm of dreams. He doesn't care whether you are ignorant or not. And he will do everything to keep you ignorant as long as he can continue to cause havoc in every area of your life.

DREAM SYMBOLS

I have decided to outline some dream symbols and their meanings only to give you some basic knowledge of the workings of satanic dreams. A lot of things in the areas of deliverance and spiritual warfare may appear unintelligible to the mind of man but nonetheless, many people are suffering untold agony from the hands of satanic agents who attacked them through dreams. Many people have personally come to see me to narrate how their problems started through some strange dream experiences. By the grace of God, we have led thousands of people into deliverance and victory. We may not touch your particular experience in this booklet, but you will gain some helpful insights into how Satan uses dreams to attack men and women.

DEEP AND MYSTERIOUS - DREAMS AND THEIR MEANINGS

* *Seeing stagnant water* reprensents lack of moving of the Holy Spirit and stagnant progress. Reveiw your spiritual life and pray against the spirit of lukewarmness.

* *Dirty water* represents the flesh and spiritual dirtiness.

* *Hair* represents the glory of God. Therefore, removal of hair in any form should be aggressively addressed.

* *Begging for alms*. This is the plan of the devil to prevent the person from getting out of an unemployed state or poverty.

* *Travelling on an unending journey* represents unprofitable endeavours. Ask the Holy Spirit to terminate all unprofitable endeavours.

* *Being driven by unknown persons to unknown destination*. This represents profitless and confused life. Ask the Holy Spirit to unseat all unprofitable drivers and make His way plain before your face.

* *Doors closing just before you enter; distribution of items finishing just before it is your turn*, etc. This represents the spirit of "almost there". Begin serious warfare praying against blockages at the edge of miracles.

* The underlisted dreams indicate that you are under attack by the *spirit of poverty*:
  - *spening money lavishly*
  - *seeing yourself buying things in the market, especially after a physical financial; breakthrough*
  - *wearing of rags or tattered shoes*
  - *walking about barefootedly*

- *seeing onself begging for alms*
- *having wares or merchadise unsold*
- *seeing your property being auctioned*
- *seeing your pockets leaking*
- *lost substantial amount of money and never found it*
- *thieves breaking into the house stealing things*
- *victim of pickpockets*
- *seeing rats running about in your house*
- *seeing rats running into your body*
- *your properties go missing*
- *your bag or purse containing money is stolen*
- *you found yourself with conuterfeit money*

* *Always sitting for examinations never finishing before the alloted time.* Demonic stagnancy, frustration and discouragement. Declare war on ungodly delays and command success into your handiwork.

* All the underlisted dreams are dreams of *defeat and backsliding.* You must declare war against all such dreams with prayer and fasting:
  - *nightmares*
  - *death or being buried*
  - *idol-worship or consulting diviners or withc-doctors*
  - *stammering*
  - *having cancer or any other disease*
  - *insanity*
  - *loss of salvation*
  - *a man getting married to a man*
  - *weakness toward temptation*
  - *compromising holiness*
  - *consuming alcohol*

* If you find yourself losing much hair from your head in real life after a dream experience in which you found yourself in a barber's shop where your hair was been

24

barbed by force, it is an indication that your glory or your security is being removed. You have to go into spiritual warfare and recover your hair. You also have to send fire to the barber's shop in the realm of the spirit.

* *If you find yourself carrying a basket on your head in a dream*, it is an indication of a satanic plan to make you suffer loss financially. You have to send the fire of God to burn the basket and recover your lost blessings.

* *If you see bats flying in your dream*, it suggests that the devil is planning to use hypocrites and pretenders against you. You have to bind the bat and ask that the power of God should descend and consume it.

* *Generally, the animals* which most people see in their dreams represent difficulty, hardships and trouble. You should either drive the animals away or decree their death.

* *Consuming alcohol in the dream* is a symbol of being under the influence of the spirit of confusion. You have to pray that you will vomit the alcohol. You also have to expel yourself from the school of confusion.

* *When a sister is getting engaged with an unknown man in a dream*, something is amiss. If she begins to commit fornication with a strange man in her dream, she, perhaps, unknown to her, has a spirit husband. Something must be done about such a strange dream. It must be stopped through violent prayer.

* *Dreams of being abandoned* indicate satanic plans to make you lose friends and favour and also making recovery difficult. Refuse to be abandoned in Jesus' name and also claim back friends and favour.

* *Dreams having to do with abortion* indicate that the

enemy is trying to steal something good from your life before the full manifestation of the particular thing. Rebuke the enemy and reject the abortion of good things.

* *Dreams of contacts with dead parents and ancestors* indicate serious physical and spiritual illnesses and evil spiritual carry-overs. Reject evil linkage, break all evil ancestral covenants and carry-overs.

* *Dreams of being attacked by armed men* indicate that you have serious spiritual battles to fight and the presence of serious obstacles to goodness. Ask the hosts of heaven to take up the battle. Call down the fire of God to destroy the evil army.

* *If you find yourself bleeding in your dream*, it means that something good is going to come out of your life. However, this may be gradual and it may eventually lead to the loss of life. You have to command that the spirit of God should heal the wound and that there should be restoration of the blood.

* *Supposing you see corpses in your dream*, you have to stand and pray against the spirit of death.

* *If you are always dreaming of seeing cobwebs all over the place*, it is a symbol of rejection. It means that the devil is trying to render your life useless. You must send fire to the spots where the cobwebs are located and scatter the producers.

* *If you dream of seeing yourself putting on earrings* when you normally do not put them on, it is a symbol of the enemy's attempt to turn you into a slave. You have to command that the earrings should be removed and sent back to the sender.

* *Any type of wigs* which people place on their head in the

dream is a symbol of false glory. It cannot last. You have to send fire to burn it and restore your normal hair.

* *If you see yourself handcuffed in a dream*, a curse is being place over your life. In addition the enemy may be attempting to incapacitate your freedom or handiwork. You have to destroy the handcuff and return it to the sender.

* *If you frequently see yourself in funeral services*, the enemy is challenging you with the spirit of death. You have to disband the funeral service including the "pastor" who is conducting it. You should also withdraw yourself from the service. It is not of God. The people who are there are only pretending to be church members. They are all satanic agents.

* *Again, if you find yourself before great mountains which you are unable to climb*, it means that there are still obstacles for you to tackle spiritually. You have to use all available weapons until the mountain is destroyed.

* *If you find yourself in the court and you happened to be the accused*, it is also an indication that there are obstacles before you. You need to pray against the obstacles and disband the court.

* *If you see padlocks in your dreams*, it means that your blessings have been locked up. You don't need to ask for the keys. Ask for the fire of God to burn the padlocks.

* *If you see yourself in tattered clothes in your dreams*, it means that you are going to lose some good things. You should stand against such a dream The enemy has plans to put you to shame.

* *If you find crabs walking all over your body*, it shows that you are going to experience a retreat. It is a sign of

27

going backward. You should stand against it.

* *If you find yourself drinking dirty water*, your spirit is being poisoned.

* *If you also dream about swimming in dirty water*, your spirit is also being poisoned. You must pray that the blood of Jesus should enter into the water. You should also command the water to dry up.

* *If you find yourself eating in the dream*, it signifies that the enemy wants to poison your spiritual life. They may even be distributing different parts of the human flesh and you may receive it if you are dull spiritually. This is satanic.

* *If you find yourself drinking a red substance*, you might be drinking blood. You have to ask the Holy Spirit to purge you immediately. You need personal deliverance. Those who eat "Fufu", "Eba", "Yam", etc, are eating terrible poison that can cause them terrible diseases. Eating sand or dust in dreams shows that the enemy is trying to cause heaviness in your spirit.

* *If you find that you were climbing with difficulty until you woke up to discover that you were sweating, profusely*, you need to pray seriously. But if you find yourself climbing until you eventually succeeded, you should begin to praise the Lord. You are victorious. But if you climbed and you could not succeed, you should pray fervently against defeat.

* *If you drove your car in a dream in a traffic jam which stood still until you wake up*, it is symbolic of a major attempt at hindering you from getting what God wants to give you. Ask the Holy Spirit to send His dispatch rider there and clear the way for you. This kind of dream

reveals the devil's strategy against your life.

* *If a person is carrying a big load on the head and he or she is sweating under the great burden*, it means that a big load on the head of the one who dreamt about it whether he knows about it or not. Such a person must reject the load and ask the Holy Spirit to remove the load from his or her head. The person can also cover himself or herself with the Blood of Jesus.

* *If you find yourself somewhere and you are told: "Look! this load belongs to you"* and you struggle endlessly without being able to lift up the load, you need to pray fervently. It means that the devil does not want you to fulfill your responsibility.

* *If you find yourself cooking beans in a dream and you cook for hours on end without the beans getting done*, you should not take it lightly. It symbolises some hindrances to receiving your goodness. You should pray that the Holy Spirit should cook the food for you.

* *If you also find yourself travelling in your dream and the vehicle in which you are travelling breaks down, and you kept on repairing it, but in spite of your efforts you could not finish the repairs before waking up*, this is an attack on the wheel of your progress. You must ask the angels of God to repair the vehicle. You must also rebuke the enemy.

* *Any form of darkness* in the dream is ominous. It represents spiritual blindness. Those who have such dreams will not see where they are going. Likewise, if you enter a vehicle or an aircraft and you begin to ask: "Where are we going?" this indicates that the enemy has dispatched the spirit of uncertainty and confusion against the individual.

* *People often see themselves receiving gun shots in the dream*. Surprisingly, bullets actually enter their body. They often feel pains when they wake up. Gun shots are evidences of affliction or satanic attack. It may eventually result into poverty or sicknesses. Demonic gun shots can easily be removed. You just remove the bullets in Jesus' name Ask the angels of God to minister treatment to you, then fire back at the source of attack.

* *If you find yourself naked in a dream*, it:is a sign of disgrace or insecurity. You must ask the Holy Spirit to clothe you and remove any object of disgrace from your life.

* *If you are putting on rags*, it is a sign of poverty and blindness. Also, if you dream of seeing yourself in chains, it is a sign of imprisonment.

* *Any form of theft in your dreams* has a deep spiritual meaning. You have to pray aggressively and claim back whatever is stolen, be it clothes, shoes, etc.

* *If you dream about people stealing your wedding dress*, it is an attack on your marital life. You must go into fasting and prayer very quickly and command the wedding gown to be returned. Then go ahead and claim God's promises for your marriage. Dreams of wedding gowns stained with blood or in rags should be aggressively dealt with.

* *If your Bible is stolen in a dream*, it is an attack on your spiritual power and ability. It is the devil's attempt to paralyse your spiritual life and eventually make you to backslide. You have to rise up and resist the devil. Pray that the Holy Spirit should return your stolen Bible and collect it by faith from the thief.

* *Dreams on getting confused* when you are supposed to share the word of God should be resisted violently.

* *Dreams concerning burglary* are spiritual attacks. You have to pray that all your property should be returned.

* *Now, in Africa mythology masquerades* are the embodiments of all evil powers. It represents the depth of satanic power. Any form of attack by masquerades should not be taken lightly at all. Masquerades are sent by witchcraft spirits and other demonic spirits. Their purpose is to disgrace you and push you into restlessness. You have to rebuke them aggressively in Jesus' name. You must paralyse their powers and use your weapon against them.

* *If you also find yourself among lodge members or if you find yourself in the midst of all kinds of people dressed in the regalia of demonic or occultic people*, it means that even in the place where you were born, you are surrounded by demonic agents. You have to fight them by commanding the fire to consume those groups of demons. Also break every conscious or unconscious covenant formed by you or formed by someone on your behalf with evil powers.

* *Any attack by dogs, cats and crocodiles* should be taken seriously.

This reminds me of a member of our church who formed the habit of praying aggressively every time. She had heard this kind of teaching. She was, therefore, sufficiently enlightened.

One day she was on her bed at home when a cat jumped in from the window and alighted on her bed. The cat bit her leg. She cried in the dream and continued doing so until she woke up. Before she woke up from the bed, the cat jumped out of the window, but as it jumped out, one leg got stucked in the window. The cat struggled and struggled until it ran out through the window,

Then when she woke up, she made her first mistake. She went to the wrong person, the oldest woman living in the house and challenged her: "Mama, my blood is bitter. If you are the cat which came to me in the dream, leave me alone. You better go and attack your own children." The woman replied: "I don't know anything about any cat. I don't know what you are talking about." Immediately the sister got to her room, her legs started getting swollen until she could no longer walk. So the sister was rushed to the hospital.

A man of God went there and told her that her case is not for the hospital. She was taken back home. The man of God then anointed the leg with oil and prayed over it. The leg began to reduce to its normal size. The pastor who ministered to her also prayed that the arrow should go back to its sender or to wherever Jesus wanted it to go. This sister was a nurse. She did not know what was really happening until she got to work and discovered that her assistant at work had a mysterious problem in one leg. This other nurse who was the brain behind the sister's attack in the dream was in a critical condition in the hospital. The Christian sister demanded to see her assistant whom she learnt was sick. She got an equally mysterious answer. The sister's assistant had given an instruction that everyone should be allowed to see her except the Christian sister. It became clear that the assistant was the culprit. She was the one who came in the form of a cat to attack the Christian sister.

In any case the sister suffered because of her ignorance of the weapons of the believer's warfare. If she had used her

God-given authority, she would not have been attacked at all.

* *If you dream and you see dogs licking your body*, you have to pray. This means you have sexual demons. You must go for deliverance if need be. Any dream concerning anybody who takes a whip and flogs you, should be taken seriously.

* *Any dream centered on receiving dirty or rough money* symbolises contermination of your finances. You have to resist and rebuke the spirit behind it and destroy the money.

* *If you find yourself in the market in your dream, just roaming about without even remembering what to buy and you ended up buying nothing*, it is an evidence that you will be confused financially. You must stand against it as well as destroy the market and withdraw yourself from it.

* *Any dream concerning somebody cursing you*, shows that the devil wants to put you under affliction perpetually. It shows that there is an evil handwriting against you. You must nullify the curses through prayer. You must blot the handwriting and pray that the curse should go back to the sender.

* *It is also demonic to have any form of sexual intercourse in the dream.* This is the demon called spirit husband or spirit wife. You have to rebuke him or her in the name of the Lord. Attack this spirit with all the weapons you know about. Bind and stop the spirit from visiting you again. But be sure you are not engaged in the sin of adultery and fornication. These two sins are fertilizers for spirit wives and husbands.

* *If you have ever discovered that anytime you want to touch or start something good, a particular dream comes up which always results in rendering all your efforts futile,* you are suffering from what we call: "The Demonic Stabilizer". The dream stabilises you and keeps you at the same level. You must use the weapon of praying and fasting. This stabilizing demonic influence may not affect your entire life, but it is a hindrance to your progress and fulfillment in life. The yoke behind it should be broken.

* *It is not good to find yourself amputated in a dream.* You should pray against the spirit of death, if you have had such an experience in your dream.

* *If you find yourself in a school which is not of God,* disband the school and remove your name from their register.

When you begin to have these types of dream and you are ignorant of their implications, you might suffer unnecessarily. If you dismiss satanic dreams with a wave of the hand thinking that they are harmless, you are only deciding to allow the devil to have his way in your life. You will do yourself a lot of good if you pray against all satanic dreams.

In conclusion, whenever you have any of these dreams, you must pray and handle such things seriously. Do not give room to the devil.

Be systematic in your dealings with satanic dreams. If you are a child of God, you are not supposed to experience satanic dreams, but if you have had them as a result of ignorance, carelessness or prayerlessness, you can experience total victory. You may ask: "But I have had these types of dream for so many years without doing anything about it. Can I still rectify things and undo what Satan has done?" Yes you can. I have good news for you. There is a glorious opportunity in the spiritual world which you need to know about. If you have a cassette player you would have discovered that there are two important functions; fast forward and rewind.

Do you know that you have facilities in prayer? Do you know that you can rewind your dream experiences back to your infancy through prayers? You can counteract the effect of all the dreams you had for the past ten, twenty or thirty years. You can pray in this manner: "Father, in the name of Jesus, I reverse the effect of the negative dreams I had ten years ago. Any negative effect should be completely cancelled by the blood of Jesus. In Jesus' name, Amen. "

If there are dreams you have forgotten, you can ask the Holy Spirit to bring the important ones to your remembrance. After recalling the dreams, you can then go ahead to cancel their negative impact upon your life.

A PRACTICAL SESSION

This booklet will not be complete without this practical session. The Bible says:

"But be ye doers of the word, and not hearers only, deceiving your own selves" (James 1:22).

There is, therefore, no way your practical benefit from the content of this booklet can be guaranteed without carrying out the following instructions.

On the one hand, it is possible to read about great peace without experiencing any iota of peace. It is also possible to read about prosperity without experiencing it. In the same vein, you can discover the secrets of satanic dreams and you can continue to suffer harassments, defeats, attacks and afflictions through dreams. But on the other hand, you can tell the devil: "Enough Is Enough"

You can tell him that you are done with satanic dreams. You can only do this effectively by taking the following steps:

ONE You must give your life to Christ and experience the new birth. When you take this step, you will experience a major lift from the level of defeat to the level of dominion. The Bible says:

"Who hath delivered us from the power of darkness, and hath translated us into the Kingdom of His dear Son: In whom we have redemption through His Blood, even the forgiveness of sins" (Colossians 1:13,14).

TWO You must pray fervently as instructed below. Prayer changes things. Prayer can change your dreams, too. Significantly, prayer removes the hands of the devil from your dreams.

THREE Get personal practical help. In most cases, you may need person-to-person counselling. Thousands of lives have been transformed through counselling and prayer. We counsel and pray for people every week. Your spiritual problem is our concern. If you were attacked in your dream, never panic when you wake up. Cooly and calmly, even if your body is vibrating with fear, take the offensive. Use the name of Jesus as your combination shield and battering ram. Plead the Blood of Jesus and claim protection against the hosts of darkness. Rebuke satan and take authority over him and his wicked followers in the name of Jesus. Be persistent. ANY REGULAR DREAM SHOULD BE GIVEN PROPER ATTENTION. It may be a pointer to the way of solution to a particular problem. Be assured that the devil and his cohorts are behind all the horrible experiences in dreams like eating with the dead, swimming in water, serving people you do not know, playing with snakes, marriage in the spirit world with unknown men or women, having children in the spirit world, having sexual intercourse with known or unknown partners, getting out of the body for meetings, forceful sex or feeding, regular drinking of red liquid, being on a throne with unknown or known faces worshiping or bowing down to you and presence in unholy parties etc.

Finally, prepare your heart now for the practical session below.

PRAYER POINTS

Go on your knees and pray the following points:

1. I claim all the good things which God has revealed to me through dreams. I reject all bad and satanic dreams in the name of Jesus.

2. (You are going to be specific here. Place your hand on your chest and talk to God specifically about the dreams which need to be cancelled. Cancel it with all your strength. If it needs fire, command the fire of God to bum it to ashes.)

3. O Lord, perform the necessary surgical operation in my life and change all that had gone wrong in the spirit world.

4. I claim back all the good things which I have lost as a result of defeat and attacks in my dreams in Jesus' name.

5. I arrest every spiritual attacker and paralyse their

activities in my life in the name of Jesus.

6. I retrieve my stolen virtues, goodness and blessings in Jesus' name.

7. Let all satanic manipulations through dreams be dissolved in Jesus' name.

8. Let all arrows, gunshots, wounds, harassment, opposition in dreams return to the sender in the name of Jesus.

9. I reject every evil spiritual load placed on me through dreams in Jesus' name.

10. All spiritual animals (cats, dogs, snakes, crocodiles) paraded against me should be chained and return to the senders in the name of Jesus.

11. Holy Ghost, purge my intestine and my blood from satanic foods and injections.

12. I break every evil covenant and initiation through dreams in the name of Jesus.

13. I disband all the hosts of darkness set against me in the name of Jesus.

14. Every evil imagination and plan contrary to my life should fail woefully in the name of Jesus.

15. Every doorway and ladder to satanic invasion in my life should be abolished forever by the Blood of Jesus.

16. I loose myself from curses, hexes, spells, bewitchment and evil domination directed against me through dreams in the name of Jesus.

17. I command you ungodly powers, release me in the name of Jesus.

18. Let all past satanic defeats in the dream be converted to victory in the name of Jesus

19. Let all test in the dream be converted to testimonies in Jesus' name.

20. Let all trials in the dream be converted to triumphs in Jesus' name.

21. Let all failures in the dream be converted to success in Jesus' name

22. Let all scars in the dream be converted to stars in Jesus' name.

23. Let all bondage in the dream be converted to freedom in Jesus' name.

24. Let all losses in the dream be converted to gains in Jesus' name.

25. Let all opposition in the dream be converted to victory in Jesus' name.

26. Let all weaknesses in the dream be converted to strength in Jesus' name.

27. Let all negative in the dream be converted to positive in Jesus' name.

28. I release myself from every infirmity introduced into my life through dreams in the name of Jesus.

29. Let all attempts by the enemy to deceive me through dreams fail woefully in the name of Jesus.

30. I reject evil spiritual husband, wife, children, marriage, engagement, trading, pursuit, ornament, money, friend, relative, etc. in the name of Jesus.

31. Lord Jesus, wash my spiritual eyes, ears and mouth with

Your blood.

32. The God who answereth by fire should answer by fire whenever any spiritual attacker comes against me.

33. Lord Jesus, replace all satanic dreams with heavenly visions and divinely-inspired dreams.

35. Confess these scriptures out loud: Psalm 27:1-2, 1Cor. 10:21, Psalm 91

36. I command every evil plantation in my life, come out with all your roots in the name of Jesus! *(Lay your hands on your stomach and keep repeating the emphasized area.)*

37. Evil strangers in my body, come all the way out of your hiding places in the name of Jesus.

38. I disconnect any conscious or unconscious linkage with demonic caterers in the name of Jesus.

39. Let all avenues of eating or drinking spiritual poisons be closed in the name of Jesus.

40. I cough out and vomit any food eaten from the table of the devil in the name of Jesus. *(Cough them out and vomit them in faith. Prime the expulsion).*

41. Let all negative materials circulating in my blood stream be evacuated in the name of Jesus.

42. I drink the blood of Jesus. *(Physically swallow and drink it in faith. Keep doing this for some time).*

43. Let all evil spiritual feeders warring against me drink their own blood and eat their own flesh.

44. I command all demonic food utensils fashioned against me to be roasted in the name of Jesus.

45. Holy Ghost fire, circulate all over my body.

46. I command all physical poisons inside my system to be neutralized in the name of Jesus.

47. Let all evil assignments fashioned against me through the mouth gate be nullified in the name of Jesus.

48. Let all spiritual problems attached to any hour of the night be cancelled in the name of Jesus. (*Pick the periods from 12 midnight down to 6:00 a.m*).

49. Bread of heaven, fill me till I want no more.

50. Let all catering equipment of evil caterers attached to me be destroyed in the name of Jesus.

51. I command my digestive system to reject every evil command in the name of Jesus.

52. Let all satanic designs of oppression against me in dreams and visions be frustrated in the name of Jesus.

53. I remove my name from the register of evil feeders with the blood of Jesus.

54. Let the habitation of evil caterers become desolate in the name of Jesus.

55. I paralyse the spirit that brings bad dreams to me in the name of Jesus.

56. Let the fire of the Holy Ghost destroy any evil list containing my name in the name of Jesus.

57. Let the fire of the Holy Ghost destroy any of my pictures in the air, land and sea in the name of Jesus.

58. I destroy any coffin prepared for me in the name of Jesus.

59. I cancel and wipe off all evil dreams in the name of Jesus.

60. I destroy every satanic accident organised for my sake in the name of Jesus.

61. I render all evil night creatures powerless in the name of Jesus.

62. Let the blood of Jesus wash all the organs in my body in the name of Jesus.

63. Let all sicknesses planted in my life throw evil spiritual food be destroyed in the name of Jesus.

64. Let the blood of Jesus erase all evil dreams in the name of Jesus.

65. Let the fire of God boil all rivers harbouring unfriendly demons in the name of Jesus.

66. Let all evil dreams be replaced with blessings in the name of Jesus.

67. I command all my good dreams to come to pass in the name of Jesus.

68. Father, hasten the performance of my good dreams.

O Lord, I thank You for another moment like this. I know that You will deliver many people in demonstration of Your Mighty power. I know that the devil is in trouble as a result of this teaching. Father, I pray that You grant every reader of this booklet the grace to be on fire at all times so that all satanic strategies against them in their dreams will be cancelled. Lord, release Your fire in the name of Jesus. I pray for those who have suffered defeat as a result of bad dreams. I decree a complete reversal of all satanic curses in Jesus' name. Let every negative situation be changed to a positive situation in the name of Jesus. I destroy every

work of the devil. Eternal Rock of Ages, we thank You. In
Jesus' name we prayed. Amen.

Made in the USA
Coppell, TX
01 November 2023

23688240R00028